Blowing Smoke

THE **WILD** AND **WHIMSICAL**

WORLD OF CIGARS

Blowing Smoke

THE WILD AND WHIMSICAL WORLD OF CIGARS

BY BRIAN MCCONNACHIE

TRIUMPH
BOOKS
CHICAGO

Printed in the United States of America.

This book is available in quantity at special discounts for your group or organization. For more information, contact:

Triumph Books
644 South Clark Street
Chicago, Illinois 60605
(312) 939-3330 Fax (312) 663-3557

Book design by Mike Mulligan.
Cover design by Mark Anderson.
Interior illustrations by Jack Ohman.

ISBN 1-57243-229-2

Dedication: To **Sam Gross,** who taught me how to spit, curse, roll drunks, and a thing or two about cigars.

INTRODUCTION

Ah! Cigars. How many powerful memories, pleasures, and images does that potent word evoke? Ever since Columbus returned to Spain with this exotic treasure from the New World, everyone—from poets to politicians, handmaidens to foot specialists, emperors to barrel designers, well diggers to canary salesmen—has been endlessly searching to perfectly describe the unique and ineffable experience of smoking an entire cigar.

Cigars have been called everything from the Brown Key of Utopian Bliss on a bed of Enchanted Ecstasy with a side order of Nirvana to Satan's doodle-stick. Charles Dickens was once heard to utter, "It's like gathering all that is comforting, warm and eternal, yes, the very essence of the campfire if you will, and putting it in your mouth where everything good and interesting eventually winds up."

Whether the activity is political, religious, or sexual, over the years, it seems the cigar has more often been the distinctive witness and welcomed guest. Indeed, it's more the exception that during events of consequence, the cigar is absent.

And its influences were never lost on women. Catherine the Great declared any man who doesn't partake in cigar smoking to be nothing more than a weak-willed, meandering oaf and swore she would never put her lips to those of any creature, man, or beast, whose lips were not fresh awash in the currents of cigar odor.

Though not a smoker herself, Queen Victoria always carried around a lit one, usually an Upmann, that she would, with great relish, twist into the back of the hand (and sometimes the buttocks), of those members of the House of Commons who tended to find fault with her policies.

CLOSET CIGAR SMOKERS
WE'D LIKE TO SEE...

Even the great thinker and reformer, Martin Luther, was not immune to the powerful allure of the tobacco leaf. When he first petitioned the Pope to reconsider many of the exploitative positions the Church was enforcing, he declared that if change was not forthcoming he would be left no choice but to sever all ties with Rome. But then added: *Mas de gustubus don et eurium Haban Bolivar fuma* (but I'll certainly reconsider if you'll be more forthcoming with some good cigars).

Indeed, it was the common policy then for the Pope to keep all the superior cigars for himself and his friends in the Holy See and dispense the inferior brands to the outer reaches of the Roman Empire. The Pope replied: *Deo non factum labouratum* (Good luck in your new job).

Then of course there is the remarkable story of General Don Vegas de La Ortegis, liberator and cigar smoker.

When a sudden change of authority placed this brave soldier and national hero in front of a firing squad, he was offered a last request and unhesitatingly shouted, "I want a fine cigar!" which he was then given.

As the members of the firing squad patiently waited and enviously watched him **savoring his last earthly pleasure,** they demanded to know, if the condemned can have a cigar, why couldn't they who would soon be doing the actual work? Were they not deserving of a fine cigar as well?

After a good deal of arguing and insisting, the captain of the guard relented and provided each of them with a cigar. But by the time the firing squad was lighting up, the General was finishing his. As he was waiting for them to be done, he asked if he might have another as it would now be some time before the soldiers would finish theirs.

The captain of the guard, an admirer of the General since childhood, could not refuse him. But by the time the squad had finished, the General was only beginning and they began demanding another round.

It was almost two thirty in the morning before they got around to shooting him.

Ah! Cigars.

Looking for a good foot-stomping opera to see with the guys? Try *Carmen*. It takes place outside of a cigar factory and has lots of chicks too.

Try not to coordinate your cigar wrapper with your watchband. Or vice versa. Your friends will think you don't have a life.

*Don't forget all those cigar smokers
on your pay-back list with thoughtful, swell,
and practical gift items like:*

THE EXACTO-METER®

A magic gauge you simply stick into your cigar, like a meat thermometer, and it tells you a host of valuable and fascinating things: how much smoking pleasure is left, the exact temperature your cigar is burning at, the approximate time you should be lighting up your next one. Plus the date, a barometer, a windchill index, the DOW, your horoscope, and the time in London, Bora Bora, and Kowloon.

INSTANT ATMOSPHERE O' GRANDE

You're having some important friends over and the well-intentioned but unknowing maid has just fumigated the place. What to do? Well, now there's Atmosphere O' Grande. It's cigar smoke in an aerosol can. It comes in several intoxicating and exotic flavors: Ringside, Poker Game, Billiard Room, Live Sex Show, Tammany Hall, and Cock Fight.

THE DREAMDOME®

At long last, someone has finally invented a device that allows you to smoke in your sleep! It's about time. How often have you told yourself: I should go to bed now. But then you say: No. I want to stay up and have another cigar. Or several.

If you can't get enough of those delicious aromas swirling around your head, just put on the DreamDome®, get in your pajamas, and catch that last boat to Dreamland. Enjoy the encapsulated fragrances of your favorite cigars while the patented Macro-Tru Valve® makes sure there is always enough ozone and oxygen to prevent suffocation.

POOL SIDE® HAPPY TIMES™ INFLATABLE CIGAR FLOAT

A fun gift the whole family can enjoy. Is it a six foot cigar? Or is it an inflatable rubber raft that wishes it were a six foot cigar? Well, it's BOTH!

Not to be used as a life preserver.

THE HELMET OF HAPPINESS®

Perfect for that person of sudden mood changes and quick decisions. One minute you can be enjoying the nut and coffee flavor of a Corona Grande and the next the creamy fun of a Jeroboam. **Comes fully loaded** with twelve different exotic cigars and color-coded sucking tubes. Also includes replaceable mouthpieces if your friends would care to gather around and partake. You could all walk down the street together.

THE RAIN MAN®

You won't have to make this troubling decision anymore: shall I take a shower or have a cigar? because now you can do both with the Rain Man®. Guaranteed to keep your cigar high and dry while you scrub and lather away to your own personal standards as you enjoy the unequaled and unique pleasure of total moisture mingled with the herbal aromatic character of a fine cigar. Also available: Smoke-scented soap.

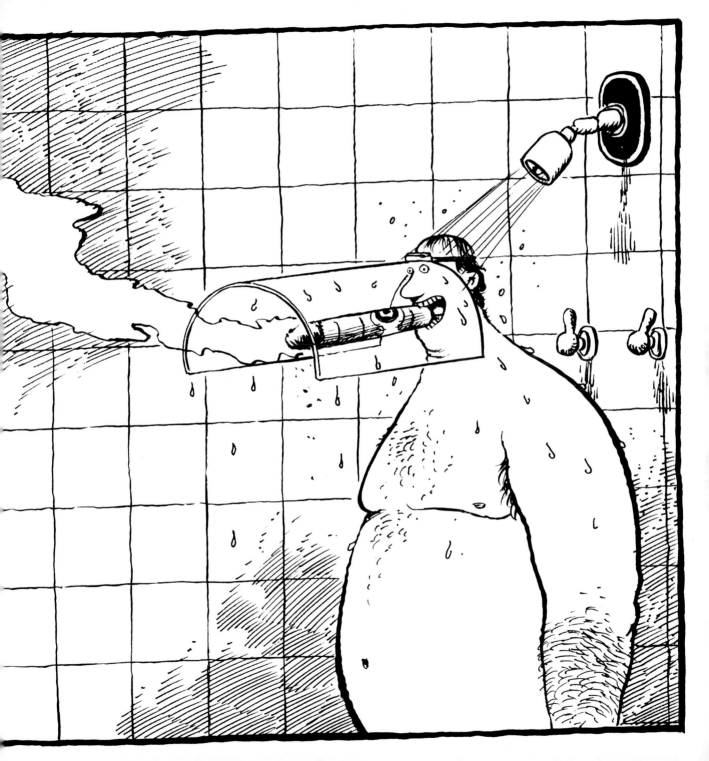

ASH-O-RAMA®

Certainly your hands have better things to do than continually knocking off the finished end of your favorite La Corona. Well here's a chance to free them up for more important matters because Ash-O-Rama® is there for you! A gentle but firm suction device fastens Ash-O-Rama® right to your jaw. When Ash-O-Rama® is full, slowly peel Ash-O-Rama® from your face and empty into a proper receptacle. For people without sufficient jaw mass or unusually oily skin, Ash-O-Rama® is also available with ear clips or a stylish neck attachment.

MY First TIME

THAT'S WHAT HAPPENED, OR WHATEVER...

"Bob Dole smoked his first cigar during World War II. He had this little side business going where we'd trade whiskey to the Japanese for prostitutes. Well one time, we were clean out of whiskey and Bob Dole thinks to himself, what else have we got? The only other thing they seemed interested in were troop movements. Now Bob Dole is not the kind of guy to let our boys down; they were getting to really depend on these prostitutes. But I was determined to bargain up. Usually we'd get forty women for a case so I demanded eighty. I would have settled for fifty. This little colonel I'm dealing with then grabs my hand and then squeezes it so hard he breaks every bone in it. Then we had cigars all around to cinch the deal. I had to smoke it with my left."

Pete Rose. "We're playing the Cardinals and my pitcher walks two guys and then gives up back to back home runs—one of them to their pitcher. But we're still up by two runs. I pick up the bullpen phone and who's on the other end but my bookie! I tell him to send in John Franco. He says no, that's not going to happen. He wants to save him for tomorrow against the Braves. I start to yell 'Who the hell is running this club?' He tells me to calm down. It's only a game, for God's sake. Stay with the pitcher you've got, he tells me. Relax. Why don't you smoke a cigar? So I get a cigar, a Dutch Master. Nice. We lost by six runs but the cigar really did relax me. I liked it."

HOW TO LIGHT A CIGAR:

WRONG RIGHT

New Celebrity Designer Cigars

As more celebrities become savvy to the perks of lending their names to clothing lines, perfumes, and restaurant chains, a lot of them are dashing to cash in on the cigar craze while they still can. Among the more visible new names are:

THE LIZ TAYLOR
Julieta y Fortenskys

On the down side, they smell funny. Like there's formaldehyde in them and then some kind of perfume was used to cover it up. They burn rather quickly, but on the plus side, they don't cost that much. A portion of the proceeds from all purchases goes to help fight pink eye, which ironically is caused by smoking these cigars in the first place.

Dear Captain Smokey,

I'm a devout Catholic, an avid cigar smoker, and head of proctology at a major metropolitan university hospital. I devote all of my remaining time to dancing at an erotic club that caters to women over forty. I guess my question is: How do I do all this and still have time to smoke a box of cigars a week? (My quota.) I certainly can't smoke in church. And I know darn well I better not have a lit cigar anywhere near where I'm examining people. That only leaves my exotic dancing, but it's real awkward. I have to pull the clothes over my head and do these leaps and spins and really need my hands. Any thoughts?

                              Busy-Busy
                              Dallas, Texas

Dear Busy,

Well, I'll tell you what I tell every proctologist I hear from: You people really earn your money. I swear to God! I don't begrudge you your fancy cars. Your big houses. Your $3,000 suits. That's what you people want to do for money, take the money.

Why don't you just wear pull-away clothes that don't have to go over your head? Or you might want to check out the new issue of *Holy Smoke*. They often list a number of cigar-friendly churches that have special smoking sections. Happy puffing.

The Cuban auto industry (1966-67) was a

short-lived venture that produced a total of 83 cars. Playing to their strengths of knowing a lot more about cigars than they did cars, they made the unique interior an actual humidor. But the elaborate cooling system was such a drain on the two cylinder engine that top speeds rarely exceeded eleven miles an hour. (Being totally bulletproof was its main selling point.)

Its biggest drawback, certainly for the Cubans, was that it was so chilly inside that

owners had to wear fur coats when they drove and many of them caught colds.

CIGARS 'N' CARS

'59 FORD EDSELS 'N' WHITE OWLS...

During the 1980s, the withering U.S. auto industry began frantically looking for quick fixes for its sagging sales. Prices were slashed dramatically but things still weren't turning around. More and more dealers were concocting come-on gimmicks to lure customers into their showrooms. One dealership in Alexandria, Virginia, began offering a box of El Producto Escepcionales to anyone who would **come in for a test drive.** This got sudden results and each day the crowds grew larger. The dealer bought up all the Escepcionales he could lay his hands on. Sales did improve but not dramatically.

One morning, as he was opening up his dealership, he noticed a lot of the same faces on the line that wound around the block. The BIG idea hit him: sell the cigars and give the cars away. For every box of Escepcionales you bought at $11,659, you would get a 1985 Oldsmobile as a bonus. He hit gold!

CIGARS 'N' CARS

WHAT TO DRIVE WITH WHICH CIGAR...

EL CAMINOS AND TIPARILLOS...

You'll want to collect and trade fun bumper stickers like:

CIGAR SMOKERS
DO IT LONGER

SNAPPY SEAGAR SEZ...

That next to his cats (he had over fifty-two of them), Ernest Hemingway loved a cigar almost as much as he loved wearing his purple muumuu and straw shade bonnet. The shade bonnet had a pale blue ribbon chin tie. If he couldn't find his favorite shade bonnet, or if his pale blue ribbon chin tie was soiled, he used a parasol. He'd smoke his favorite, a Montechristo, stroll along twirling his parasol, and with one of his cats tucked in the crook of his arm, sing to it. He'd sing songs like "Night and Day" and "When They Begin the Beguine" or "I've Got You Under My Skin." He always knew how to have a wonderful time by himself. Just smoking cigars, twirling his parasol, singing Cole Porter songs to his cats—Ernest Hemingway! Why would a man who had all that want to take his own life? It remains still a mystery.

My First Time

Dick Clark. "My first cigar. Let's see. Coolidge was in the White House. The economy was flying along. I'm walking down the street with no particular destination in mind. But then I realize I'm almost forty-six. What do I want to do with my life?

'Why don't you smoke a cigar?' says a voice in my head. So I got a cigar, a Presidente. Smooth. I was standing there puffing away and I'm thinking to myself: what I am going to do the rest of my life? What do I like to do? I wasn't sure, so I took another puff.

Then it hit me—I love to watch teenagers dance. They are so full of life, jumping all around. But how do you make money doing that? I didn't know then but I knew I better figure it out soon. You don't live forever, I said to myself. Boy, was I off on that one!"

Mike Nichols

"Unfortunately, the first and last cigar I ever had was a particularly powerful exploding cigar. I can't imagine what the person who packed it was thinking. When it blew up, I burned all the hair off of my body. Now I have to wear all these different little wigs. Some joke!"

Dear Captain Smokey,

I had just put Microsoft Windows '95 into my computer and the whole thing just goes kerplouie. Down. Gone. Done. I lost everything. EVERYTHING! Eighteen months of research and work. I couldn't believe it. I wanted to STRANGLE Bill Gates with my bare hands. So I'm in a bar and this guy comes over and very dramatically produces a cigar from a tube and offers it to me. It wasn't labeled. He said it was a WISH cigar. I smoked it, made a wish, and calmed down. It was quite good.

Now about a month after that, Bill Gates is dedicating some new wing at the Seattle zoo when all of a sudden two chimps start slapping him and pounding him in the head. Unbelievable! Now I know I probably should have wished all my work would come back but instead I had wished Bill Gates would get beaten to death with animal bones by Barbary apes. Now this wasn't exactly that but you can see it's certainly in the right direction. How can I get more WISH cigars and finish the job?

> Ready for Closure
> University of Washington

Dear Ready,
WISH cigars are rare. You were lucky. They are made in Haiti by voodoo specialists and depending on the *gris-gris* content, your wish will be totally or only partially granted. They actually have a web site but I guess it wouldn't do you any good, would it?

CIGARS 'N' FISHING

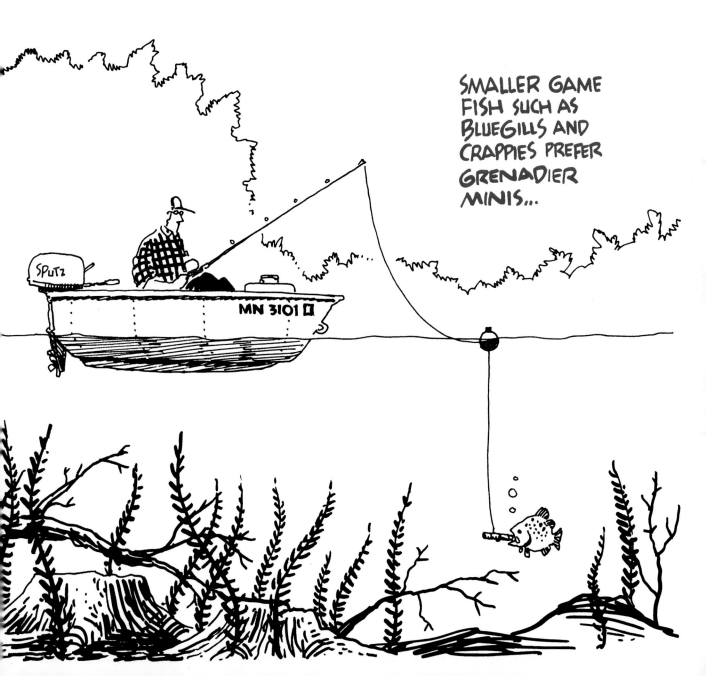

New Celebrity Designer Cigars

BILL CLINTON'S

Donde Está Mi Dinero

This is a first for a sitting U.S. president to lend his name to a commercial product, but as he puts it: "Like many of my fellow Americans, I've got bills to pay. I'm just trying to get by like everybody else. I just don't know where my paycheck goes." Actually, it has quite a smooth draw, but for its size, the amount of smoke this cigar gives off is inconceivable.

New Cigar Magazines

The staying power of any new trend can be measured by how many magazines spring up claiming to speak for the subject. No fewer than six hundred and eighty-seven cigar-related magazines have been published since 1995. Among the most promising remain:

Big Butts

Upscale stroke book featuring overweight society girls who pose bare-ass with cigars. (Jim Carey provided all the start-up money.) A lot of these women claim they do it to embarrass their rich, uncaring families by dragging their names through the mud.

Elusive Cigar Life

Each month has a brand new list of the best, most exclusive cigars in the world. All of which are virtually impossible to come by. Cigars are rolled on the sweaty thighs of virgin Dominican nuns as they listen to Ravel's *Bolero* while dirty passages from Father Greeley novels are read to them.

Cigar Seriamente

A magazine for very, Very, VERY serious cigar smokers. All text. Each issue is a different 80,000 word essay on topics like: "Can Horse Laxatives Correct Potential Soil Irregularities in Emerging Third World Tobacco Growing Nations?" "Why Is There No Tobacco in Saskatoon?" Written in old Spanish. No pictures. $26.95 an issue. Not for everyone.

Gay Alternative Smoke Style

Publishes the most comprehensive list of cigar-friendly resorts, weight rooms, coffee houses, public baths, antique stores, cruise lines, counties, cities, nations, and continents.

Holy Smoke

For high-end church and synagogue officials. Christians and Jews now have a lot more to argue about than they ever realized. Who first discovered the goodness of cigars? Is there one true cigar? Did God really give Moses a box of cigars along with the Commandments? If so, why didn't he share them?

Nudist Cigar World

Founded to support the nudist creed "A Cigar IS Just A Cigar, Damn It!," this magazine goes to considerable lengths to make this point. At least three to five features in every issue belabor the dissimilarities between cigars and other like-shaped objects. A lot of side-by-side photo spreads captioned: "This is a cigar; this is NOT a cigar."

Puff-Puff Chew-Chew

Aimed at men and women who can't decide between chewing tobacco and cigar smoking so they do both at once. Very busy, messy, gooey, yucky layout.

Perfect Rings

Aimed at middle-income newlyweds who have taken up cigar smoking together, or are planning to. Everything revolves around the cigar. Bride and groom exchange wrapper bands in special ceremony. Cute, fuzzy stuff.

The Simple Cigar Life

Rather low key accounts of ordinary men and women who smoke cigars while doing other things like laundry, painting their nails, reading the mail, getting the oil changed, listening to the radio, writing checks. Things like that. Very real, but ultimately quite eerie.

Cigars & Bathrooms & Kitchens

Smart home design for modern-thinking, cigar-loving couples who want to define the areas designated for cigar smoking. For those who want to say: "This is not only my kitchen, it's my walk-in humidor with an eat-in breakfast nook."

Eve's Leaf

Cigar magazine for independent cigar smoking women of high style and fashion. Features articles on how to color coordinate outfits with different tobacco shades. What wrappers go best with what eye liner.

Incredible but True Cigar Stories

Outlandish, bogus accounts of cigar smokers who lie about how much money they make, the size of body parts, how many women they've had at once, and then always manage to stick someone else with the bill. They unwind by climbing into the cockpit of their new untested jet, lighting up, and taking her out for a spin.

The Humordoor

A monthly collection of comical after-dinner stories and jokes that cigar smokers seem partial to. How many cigar smokers does it take to replace a light bulb? One. And he'll usually instruct the porter to do it.

Ashtray News

Ashtrays are back and bigger than ever. Looks like *People* magazine but with ashtrays. Features styles, trends, sizes, new space age metals. Rags to riches stories of top designers. Some are smaller than thimbles; you'd need a couple dozen to take care of one cigar. Some are huge, enormous things. Some are so big, they have chairs and tables in them.

Some Also-Rans

Promising cigar magazines that did not survive their first year.

Absolutely Amazing Cigar Stories

True accounts of uncommonly brave men and women who have risked their lives to rescue others and refused any reward beyond having a cigar. It became the basis of the popular TV series, "Emergency Rescue 911," but they dropped the cigar part.

Dada? Ga ba!

An avant-garde attempt to capture the cigar smokers of the art world. However, the magazine was shaped like an actual cigar which seriously limited its content. But of all the Haiku poetry devoted to cigar smoking, it was undoubtedly publishing the best.

Kick Me! Burn Me!

Appealed to aficionados of rough cigar stuff. K-B ran an incredibly detailed article on which cigars left which types of burns on which types of skin. And what kind of makeup would hide it. It was always popular with dermatologists.

Cigars from Mars

Science fact and fiction of what cigar smoking would be like in outer space. In zero gravity and beyond!

New Celebrity Designer Cigars

MADONNA'S
El Erecto-mentes and La Mama Mias

This is not subtle stuff. It's what they call "high concept." Each Erecto-mente is shaped to resemble a slightly bowed eight-inch circumcised erection and comes individually wrapped in a condom. La Mama Mias, on the other hand, come with a nipple mouthpiece and a collection of Madonna's favorite lullabies and bedtime stories. The testers refused to try them as they did not consider these cigars to be a serious entry into the marketplace.

Mahatma Gandhi—a big cigar smoker. And next to cigars, he loved

filthy jokes. The filthier, the better, he'd say, slapping his palm to the table, ready for the next

one. Enema jokes always topped his list. He'd laugh so hard at enema jokes, he'd sometimes

choke. One time he laughed so hard at a particularly raunchy enema joke that he spit his cigar,

an El Rey Del Mundo, clear across the room and then his diaper fell off. That set him off laugh-

ing even more. He had to be sedated.

There was a whole section of British intelligence assigned to write enema jokes in the

hopes of keeping Gandhi distracted from establishing home rule.

Dear Captain Smokey,

A guy I know was just mangled in a car wreck. In fact, there's a video of it for sale called "Real Life Violent Crashes." I think his wreck is the third one on the tape. Well, what I'm writing about is I'm getting together a bunch of friends and we're going to have a memorial service and then smoke cigars. What would be appropriate for something like this? We all liked him. He was a good guy but he wasn't, like, anybody's best friend.

Wondering
San Bernardino, California

Dear Wondering,

This is a little ditty that's always good to remember:

> *When you're just riding around in the back of your limo*
> *That's the time to smoke, smoke, smoke the Supremo*
> *For people departed, not later, not sooner*
> *That is the time for the Double Corona.*

Cigar Advice

Always do what the important people tell you. But have your plan. Be a good Yankee boy. If they ask, say you come from Austria. Never Germany. They hate the Germans in Hollywood. But they loved the Kennedys. So if you're German, at least marry a Kennedy. Now with smoking, be careful. Germans usually smoke cigarettes with their wrist closer to their jaw. Don't try this, you'll never get work. Smoke cigars. The bigger, the more expensive, the better. Always look busy and smile. Take off your shirt quickly whenever they tell you to. Fight the bad guys. Make a lot of money but keep most of it in Deutsche marks and yen. Say "please" and "thank you." Never punch any paparazzi. Wave and smile but always stay alert. Open restaurants and feed people all the cholesterol they can eat. Pretend to want extra helpings yourself but hide it in your napkin. If they offer you their single malt scotch say, "Oh yes, please" but pour it out somewhere and say "Mmm, that was good!" Stay lean and hungry. Offer them your bigger, more expensive cigars and watch their eyes half close with pleasure. Watch their throats as they laugh at their little stupid jokes...and be patient...time is on our side...soon...our time will come.

Jack Nicholson.

"I was about ten years old when my buddy, Joey Fetchanado, comes over with a box of primo cigars and says, hey, let's go to town. Now I had just seen Pinocchio and frankly, Disney had left a very negative impression of cigar smoking with me. So I asked what else have you got? He said he knew where we could get a bottle of tequila that could make us see things we never saw before. That beat sprouting donkey ears as far as I was concerned. We went into the basement of this building and hidden in the back was the bottle of tequila. First it was fun but then I started feeling real crappy.

He said he'd heard of a sure cure. It was called LSD. Some guy kept some in one of the old trunks there. We finally found it and then things started to get real unconventional. The walls were turning into meatloaf and all the trunks and lamps started marching around the basement singing dirty bullfighting songs. Then I THINK I heard him say the only way to counter this was to steal a school bus, get some heroin and head for Canada. Somewhere along the way I think we ate the box of cigars. When we woke up in Vermont somewhere, at least our ears were normal and we didn't bray."

You don't have to be a great golfer to be great to play golf with. If you're really lousy, bring along some superior cigars and hand them out to the other players. Make prepos-terous bets that only you could lose. Pick up the tab for the drinks afterwards. Get their cars for them. If your wife is attractive, you might want to offer them some quality time with her. You'll never be wanting for golf partners again— no matter how inept you are.

CIGARS 'N' GOLF

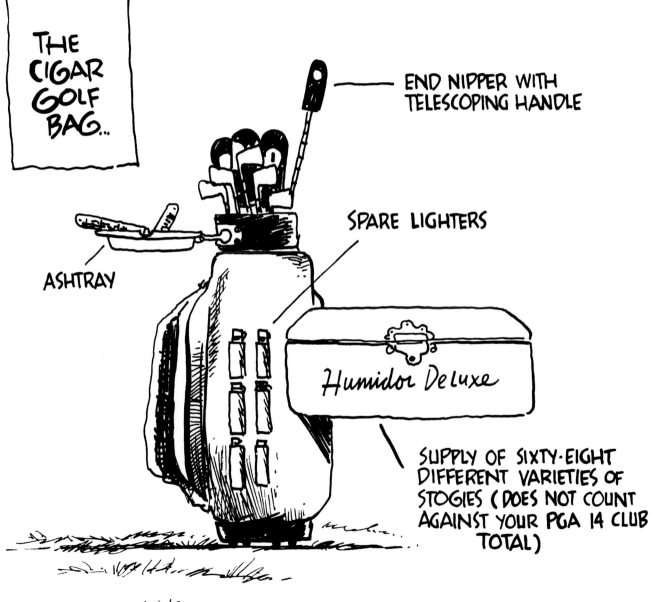

THE CIGAR GOLF BAG...

END NIPPER WITH TELESCOPING HANDLE

SPARE LIGHTERS

ASHTRAY

Humidor DeLuxe

SUPPLY OF SIXTY·EIGHT DIFFERENT VARIETIES OF STOGIES (DOES NOT COUNT AGAINST YOUR PGA 14 CLUB TOTAL)

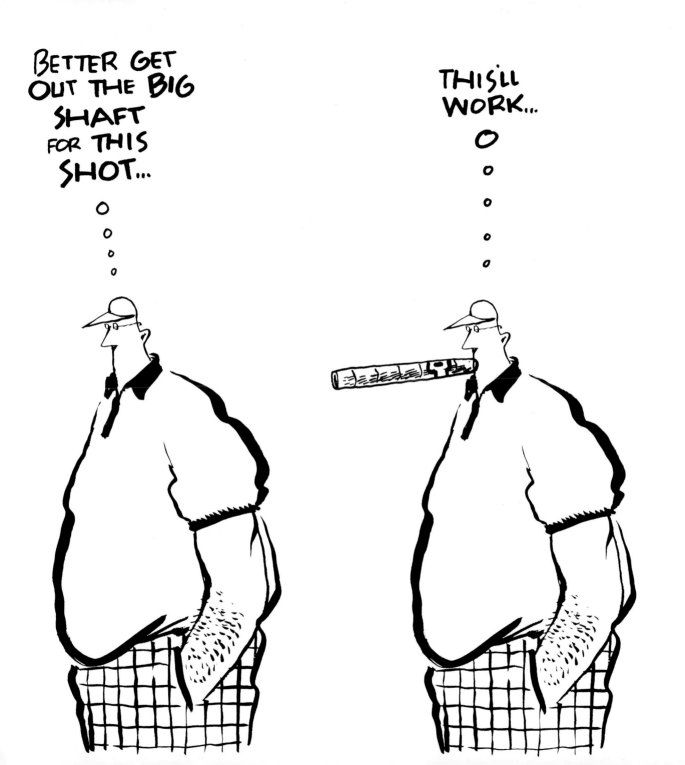

CIGARS 'N' GOLF

ANOTHER GOOD REASON TO COMBINE CIGARS AND GOLF IS THAT YOU CAN OBSCURE YOUR OPPONENT'S VISION WHEN HE PUTTS...

CIGARS 'N' GOLF

THE BEST REASON TO SMOKE CIGARS WHILE GOLFING IS TO HAVE SOMETHING TO BURN YOUR SCORECARD WITH...

Won't you try this simple Test of Life?
Match the occasion with the accessory.

Occasions:

Second mortgage

Third divorce

Prostate cancer benign

Girlfriend not pregnant

Good sex with the boss's wife

Your kid got into Yale

You won a rigged election

You're in the will

Won lawsuit against cigarette maker

Ex-wife has big tax trouble

Discover you have power over all lesbians

Sultan of Brunei wants to meet your sister/wife/daughter

The baby's a hermaphrodite

All IRS computers blow up

The DNA and the DA say it's yours

Denied club membership

What to Reach for:

A Te-Amo

A .357 magnum

A Macanudo

Your checkbook

A Montechristo

A Robusto #4

Beer nuts

Antonio y Cleopatra

Your passport

A Presidente

A gin bottle

The Polaroid

A hockey mask

A Maduro

Prozac

Beef jerky

New Celebrity Designer Cigars

My Top Twenties

Each cigar is individually numbered in descending order with the assumption that the cigar labeled ONE is going to be superior to the cigar labeled TWENTY. But that is not the case. The first two are interesting; the box peaks around FOURTEEN. Then they're all the same. ONE is actually kind of a letdown, but then you remember FOURTEEN was good and you think about that one again and smile.

AND NOW, LADIES AND GENTLEMEN, THE TOP TEN REASONS WHY YOU SHOULD BUY THESE CIGARS... NUMBER TEN..."SMELL LESS LIKE BAYONNE, NEW JERSEY THAN YOU MIGHT THINK..." NUMBER NINE..."CLEARS OUT YOUR DOG'S SINUSES..." NUMBER EIGHT...

Winston Churchill, one of the most influential and distinguished men

of this century was born Akmed Gemmelstein on the lower East Side of New York City. His mother, a diminutive, fist-waving dynamo was determined that he would have a one-way ticket out of the ghetto but his delicate constitution and ephemeral nature seemed lacking in those elements that this task required. So from the age of seven, she dressed him in suits, made him smoke cigars, and told people he was a midget. After numerous failed attempts, she managed to get him enrolled in a military school in England. He never looked back. The rest is history.

(He actually cared much less for cigars than people realized. They tended to make him dizzy, affecting his delicate constitution, but he knew he did some of his best speeches dizzy. The whole "Iron Curtain" concept came to him as he was passing out a Double Corona.)

There have been rumors that whenever he visited the White House he would drink everything in sight and run around the upstairs naked. Once, when FDR came upon him in this state, Churchill suddenly demanded to know what date the U.S. planned to enter the war. Roosevelt, hesitating to answer, found himself, wheelchair and all, being pushed down a flight of stairs. The evidence to back this up is flimsy at best.

MY First TIME

Gloria Steinem recalls the first time she smoked a cigar was at the second Firpo-Dempsey fight...

"Someone offered me a cigar, I guess as a joke. The place was really charged. It was a total crazed scene. There these two galoots were, pounding the hell out of each other. The face, the belly, the kidneys. Everyone was screaming for blood. I looked at the offered cigar, said, 'Sure, why not?,' and lit up.

It was a Corona. It was pretty smooth. I liked the way my lips fit around it.

It put me over the top. I got all wrapped up in it. Everyone in the place was doing these little jabs and uppercuts. But I have to say here, and I mean this, if one or both of the fighters were women, I wouldn't have gone. I think that's barbaric. But two half-naked men beating each other's brain to mush, I mean, really, what's not to like? Since then I've moved up to Ultimate Fighting where I'll usually smoke a Royal from the Partagas Limited Reserve. You might say I like my cigars like I like my fightin' men—bold, unrelenting, and big on the lips."

New Celebrity Designer Cigars

O. J. SIMPSON'S

Merde sur Bruno Magli
Adios a la Sangre La Morte Amore

These two lines are virtually identical and can be described as leaving a taste that is slashing, sharp, and penetrating. Any smoke that manages to drift down into the throat produces a distinct piercing sensation. Every box is personally signed and contains a little "something" from the Rockingham mansion. A spoon, a door knob, a sock. Items like that. The entire package is quite expensive. $895.00 a box.

HOW TO GET THE END OFF A CIGAR...

NO   NO

HOW TO GET THE END OFF A CIGAR, CONTINUED...

NO

HOW TO GET THE END OFF A CIGAR, CONCLUSION...

Where Are They Now?

THE MURIEL CIGAR LADY

(Edie "Why don't you pick me up and smoke me sometimes?" Adams) At the untimely death of her comic genius husband, Ernie Kovacs, Edie Adams found herself under an avalanche of debt. Not one to throw in the towel, she started digging out. Besides singing, she became an Avon lady, bred llamas, and wrestled professionally. She moved to Florida where she shared a condo with the woman who played the voice of Bambi's mother. Through her, Edie hooked up with an active group of Cuban exiles and was able to provide them with weapons and lightweight llama jackets. She was the only woman present during the Bay of Pigs invasion where she was wounded, captured, and has remained ever since in a Cuban prison.

Where Are They Now?

THE WHITE OWL

The original owl, named Mr. Perspicacity, was given to Raymond Edison Unsworth, the noted wildlife artist, to paint and then if he wished, to keep for a pet. "He was a perfect model," said Unsworth. No sooner was the work finished when Mrs. Unsworth burst into the studio with a rifle and shot the animal dead. Owls gave her the willies. The bird was then stuffed and sold at auction. Since then it has been to auction six more times, fetching approximately 28% more than it was purchased for each time. It is now held by the estate of Anna Nicole Smith.

Where Are They Now?

THE OLD DUTCH MASTERS

There were originally seven who posed for the painting and like the saying goes, **they were neither old nor Dutch,** nor masters of anything. At least at the time. One of them, Lee Trevino, however did go on and win the Masters. Two others, Peter Tork and Davy Jones, became half of the TV sensation "The Monkees." Of the remaining four, Roger Smith became the president of General Motors, Arnold Schwarzkopf rose through the ranks to the position of Joint Chief, and Sam Walton founded Walmart. But unfortunately, one of the seven has been conspicuously absent from every one of their yearly reunions: Hannibal Lecter.

SNAPPY SEAGAR SEZ...

Every day after lunch, John F. Kennedy would have a different woman snuck into the oval office. They were usually the wives of freshmen Congressmen. He preferred keeping his hands free during sex so he could read documents and smoke his après lunch Particulares by Hoyo de Monterrey. He loved its easy draw and coffee-like taste. Well, one day he's busy with a very appealing spouse of a junior member from South Carolina when he takes a drag and it suddenly plugs up on him. He almost chokes. He glares at the box it came in and without missing a beat, grabs the phone. "Castro! Shoot that bastard!"

Dear Captain Smokey,

I've been a big cigar fan for more than two years now and I can't tell you how much I love them. Can't get enough. I started with Upmans but a friend of mine said he could get me a cigar that was really fabulous. He said they were Ronda Yo Heebos or some name like that. Since I started smoking them, amazing things have been happening.

Take my dog for instance. You've never seen this--my dog can take out her left eye. She rubs it with her paw and it pops out and she looks like some crazy old prospector. She bats it around the floor for a little while then she presses her head against it and it pops back in. This isn't some Stupid Pet Trick you see on David Letterman. This is an honest to God, blow your mind, weird stuff. But she only does it when I'm smoking Ronda Yo Heebos or Ariba Ye Has or whatever they're called.

Have you heard of these? My friend has moved away. How can I get more?

Excited and Happy
Austin, Texas

Dear Excited and Happy,
I've looked through my books and I can't find that particular brand.

New Celebrity Designer Cigars

DENNIS RODMAN'S
El Loco Whackerinos

This brand was obviously rushed to the marketplace before it had any chance to age. The leaves are still green. Some common complaints from testers who tried them include: blurred vision, dizziness, serious skin and hair discoloration, hyperventilation, total disorientation, and sudden violent mood swings. Two of the testers started kicking each other in the groin for no apparent reason.

The Interview

Alonzo Gustoph Dilleghey has been a chief tobacco auctioneer for the last eighteen years. Born in 1954 in Cuba of Spanish, Irish, German, and French ancestry, he is a descendant of four generations of tobacco growers. His family fled Cuba in 1959 and resettled in Miami. He attended Stanford University and the Wharton School of Business. He holds advanced degrees in communications, music theory, and jazz composition, is fluent in five romance languages, and has mastered several different South African clicking dialects. He is head of the Linguistics Department at the University of North Carolina at Chapel Hill. He has won the Southern States of America Yodeling Championship three years running.

(Admittedly, his speech is quick and takes a little getting used to, but after a while it becomes clear.)

The interviewer is Derek Fisher, editor and publisher of Tobac-O-nomics, *the London-based journal of tobacco futures and industry gossip.*

DF: First I want to thank you for taking time from your busy schedule to grant this interview. I'll be as brief as I can because I know you have an auction in a little while. Looking back over the last ten years, what would you say are the most important changes and trends in the tobacco industry, with cigar tobacco in particular?

AD: Aut beni be deet. Nee-nay fidditda naw. Gaba dee ree bay.

DF: That's interesting you say that because that goes right to the heart of what a number of the retailers have been complaining about: keeping those kinds of cigars in stock is proving increasingly difficult. So does that mean when you say 'fidditda naw' you feel certain hydroponics will be playing a much larger role in the future of tobacco growing?

AD: Dadaw biddie deet donna fot.

DF: I'd never heard that before but that certainly could explain some of the changes in the Gulf Stream and different weather patterns over the past twenty-five years. But is that necessarily a bad thing? Isn't it in a way an evolutionary change, natural selection, if you will, that could lead eventually to superior tobacco?

AD: Cal dawt be daw doddidy da.

DF: If that's true, that's something we all can look forward to. Let's go back a little. What advice would you give to young people just starting out in the business?

AD: Delldee doe neeno badadot. Naw ne bada dee da daw.

DF: That perspiration/inspiration ratio is probably true in all businesses. Do you think it's more competitive now than when you started?

AD: Beeldle autten doofee lide Marda Stuid.

DF: THE Martha Stewart! She's making cigars now? Get out of here. Since when? Isn't her plate pretty full with house and garden tips?

AD: Nought. Ded dee bow hadley rawdimawt. Marda Stuid...and Cabbylee Gibbord.

DF: Kathy Lee Gifford too! I guess this is happening because the demand has gotten so great. But I must ask, is this in any way tied into her Honduran camps?

AD: Webb, noddy bot dillidy hobbee dee daydere. Dodo beet ray.

DF: Let me get this straight. You're saying Kathy Lee smuggles her illegal Honduran immigrants into Texas, then they go by truck all the way up into Connecticut and she turns them over to Martha Stewart who puts them to work on her farm growing wrapper tobacco?

AD: Vadee diddlie did.

DF: This is really hard to believe. Roughly speaking, how many people are we talking about here?

AD: Dip. Beedee.

DF: 300 to 400 people! And you say they all live in her barn! That's a lot of people. And you say they're too frightened to try and escape.

AD: Ceed oh bee doop.

DF: Oh no! She actually beats them with her gardening tools if they don't produce their quota! Do the other tobacco growers in the area know about this? Has anyone gone to the authorities?

AD: Dowbudy bucks wid Marda. Fee dow dee.

DF: What about Kathy Lee? If she knew Martha beat the Honduran workers so badly, she'd be outraged and wouldn't stand for it. She would stop supplying her.

AD: Caddy bo. Fidid.

DF: She knows! You mean to tell me it was actually Kathy Lee's idea to beat them with gardening tools if they acted up or complained about the Connecticut winters? And only feed them every other day! What do they get fed every other day?

AD: Keebot doddle deet bettle do dee.

DF: Lemon tarts, brown apple betty, and wedding cake! And her cooking experiments that go bad! This is just terrible. How can she expect laborers to exist on wedding cake? Do they get any protein at all to sustain their strength?

AD: Riddley rip do-da Caddy.

DF: That's absolutely criminal! So she just says there's plenty more where they come from. I know this is terrible to ask but I feel compelled to and I'm sure readers would want to know: does this result in a better wrapping tobacco?

AD: Daba diddley doot.

DF: I see. Well I guess you don't make an omelette without breaking some eggs.

AD: Gotba dee dill doot-da.

DF: Yes, I agree that is a LOT of eggs. Have the neighbors complained about the screaming? And have any of the Hondurans tried to escape or try to find employment with competitive growers?

AD: Doe.

DF: Well is there anybody else involved in this illegal activity?

AD: Betlle Strub.

DF: Sally Strouthers! My God. I would have never guessed her.

AD: Doe, Mebble Streeep.

DF: Oh, Meryl Streep.

AD: Des. Baba da net cododo lex.

DF: You say she treats her illegals much better. Well, yes. You would expect her to treat her workers well; she's an Academy Award-winning actress. She feeds them two meals a day. Considering they're better treated, do they work harder than Martha's?

AD: Yep.

DF: Is the tobacco any better?

AD: Dope.

DF: I guess this is up to the Federal authorities and the State of Connecticut to do something about this if they can.

AD: Yea ripe...da betta doe.

DF: Thank you for speaking with us. This has been most enlightening. And shocking. I guess a conclusion to draw: It's a growing, competitive, and tough business and like everything else in the real world, it does have its ugly side. And for those people who are socially concerned, until the authorities sort this out, they can always choose to boycott Martha Stewart tobacco.

AD: Gub luk.

DF: Yes, the same to you.